Praise for Spectacular Senses

"Spectacular Senses provides a fantastic workbook with activities to engage the senses, validate feelings, and teach mindfulness. It also has excellent recommendations for caregivers on additional ways to support the children in their lives. A must have for your bookshelf."
Ariel Helm, ATR-BC, LPC, Art Therapist

"Spectacular Senses is an outstanding resource to help children recognize how their senses affect the way they learn and experience the world. Megan uses an interactive and kid-friendly approach to guide children through exploring their individual sensory preferences and how to regulate them. Activities are engaging and appropriate for a wide range of ages with adult assistance. I am confident that this workbook will prove beneficial for parents, therapists, and educators seeking to help children cope with various sensory challenges." Amber Stewart, M.S. Ed., Grade 3 Teacher

"So often, parents are looking for trusted practical tools to help foster growth in their children. This book aims and excels at equipping parents with a guide to help navigate through their child's journey with the five senses. Meg Menkis gives the reader engaging activities and thoughtful discussions to be shared within the home. She does a remarkable job of pulling great resources and experiences together to help families raise young ones. I personally look forward to exploring this with my own daughter and encourage families to add this tool to their parenting toolkit. It's a fun learning experience!"
Josh Marengo, Special Ed. Teacher

Spectacular Senses

My Sensory Processing Workbook

Megan Menkis ATR-BC, LPC

Spectacular Senses

My Sensory Processing Workbook

Megan Menkis ATR-BC, LPC

MERAKI PRESS

PUBLISHING HOUSE

Additional copies may be purchased from Meraki Press.
Contact merakipress2021@gmail.com for information about bulk purchases or any other
questions.

Cover Design: Megan Menkis
Illustrator: Megan Menkis
Layout Design: Katie Zeliger of Meraki Press

Printed in the U.S.A
First Edition: October 2023
ISBN: 979-8-9873516-6-6

Megan Menkis ATR-BC, LPC
inspirecreativetherapy@gmail.com

Megan Menkis is a Licensed Professional Counselor and Board Certified Art Therapist. She has
been practicing in PA for over 5 years and has a passion for working with children and families.

Many children suffer from sensory processing disorder, but it can look different for everyone.

In this book, we will explore all 5 senses, how they work, and how you feel about them. You may find that some senses bother you more than others.

Use the pages of this book in a way that is most helpful to you! It is meant to be a guide - You can complete all or some of the pages. It may be most helpful to read through this book with a trusted adult.

Part One

All About Senses:

An Overview

What are senses?

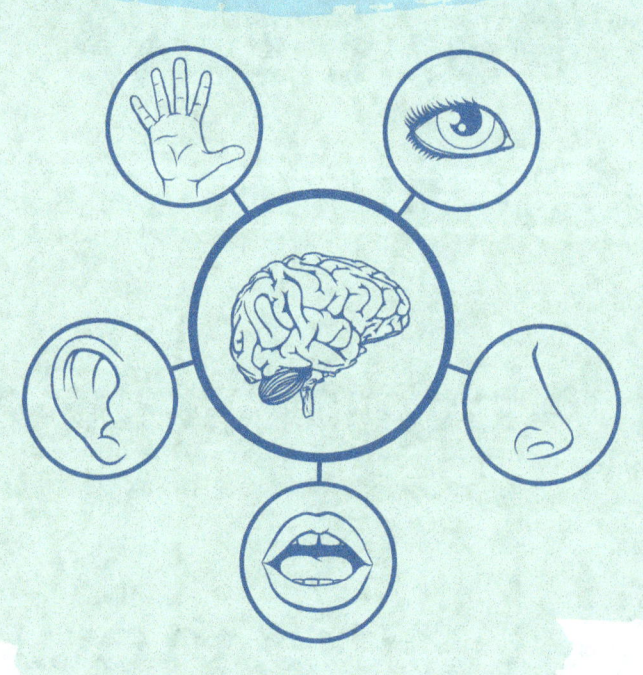

Senses are ways that your body helps you learn about the world around you. Everybody has 5 senses: sight, smell, taste, hearing, and touch.

Everyone has 5 senses:

Your eyes help you see.

Your nose helps you smell.

Your tongue helps you taste.

Your ears help you hear.

Your hands help you touch.

How Senses Work

Sight

Your pupils (the black part of the eye) use light to send signals to your brain, forming a picture of what is around you. Two parts of the eye called rods and cones have different jobs. Rods measure how bright light is, and cones help you see color!

How Senses Work

Smell

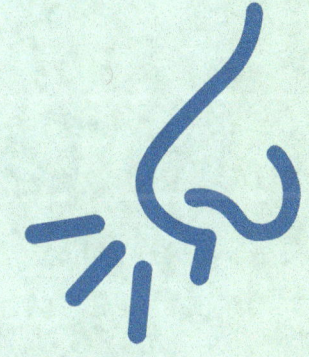

Another word for smell is "olfaction." When you smell, your nose is picking up tiny pieces of the smell floating in the air. Your nose then sends a signal to your brain, helping you decide if a smell is pleasant or not.

How Senses Work

Taste

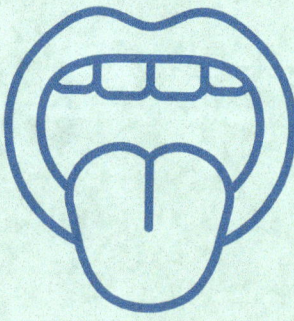

The taste buds (the little red bumps) on your tongue can help you determine if something tastes sweet, salty, sour, savory, or bitter. Everyone's taste buds are unique, which is why you may have different food preferences than your friends!

How Senses Work

Hearing

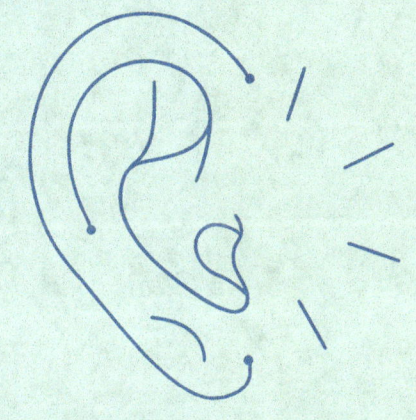

The noises we hear are actually all different vibrations in the air called sound waves. Your ear drum (inside your ear) moves at different speeds based on the sound you are hearing.

How Senses Work

Touch

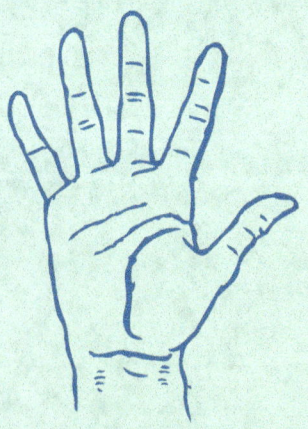

The top layer of your skin is made of special tiny parts, called cells, that help you touch. Some cells feel heat and some feel pain. Scientists are still learning about how skin sends these messages to your brain.

The things you notice with your senses are called sensations.

Everyone has sensations they like and some they don't like.

Activity

Peel an Orange

Directions:

Have a trusted adult help you peel an orange. Take a bite if you want! As you peel the orange, try to notice all the different sensations - what do you see, smell, hear, taste, and feel? Which sensations did you like? Was there any part of peeling the orange that you did not like?

Activity

Peel an Orange

Write down your observations on this page.

Did you know...

You also have two more hidden senses? You can't see them, but they are helpful ways your body and brain talk to one another about the world around you.

Pro-pri-o-cep-tion

Proprioception is a word for how your brain knows your body is moving and balancing.

Spac-i-al Or-i-en-ta-tion

Spacial Orientation is a word for how your brain knows where your body is.

There are many ways our bodies
move and balance in space!
Here are some examples:

Catching a Ball

Drawing With Crayons

Jumping Jacks

Running a Race

Playing Hopscotch

Climbing the Jungle Gym

Clapping your Hands

Can you think of any more examples?

Try some out and see how they feel!

Activity

Sensory Walk

Directions:

With a trusted adult, go on a walk around your neighborhood. Talk to your trusted adult about everything you notice. What can you see, hear, smell, feel, and taste? Which sensations are pleasant to you, and which ones are unpleasant?

Activity

Sensory Walk

Write down your observations on this page.

Part Two

Our Five Senses:

The Specifics

Sight

Fun Facts:

Your eyes see upside down, and backward. You brain adjusts the image!

Your pupils (the black part of the eye) change size depending on how much light you see.

You blink over 10,000 times a day.

Thing I love to see:

Things I do not like to see:

Activity

Blindfolded Drawing

Directions:

Have a trusted adult help blindfold you to cover up your eyes or just keep your eyes closed. On the next page, try drawing a picture with your eyes still covered up. Was it hard or easy to draw without being able to see? Did your picture turn out the way you thought it would?

Activity

Blindfolded Drawing

Draw Here

Smell

Fun Facts:

Each human has their own unique smell.

Dogs are more sensitive to smells than people.

Your sense of smell is the first sense you have, and it can help shape your emotions and memories.

Smells I love:

Smells I do not like:

Activity

Sense of Smell Game

Directions:

Have a trusted adult place several different smelly things in a muffin tin (for example, spices, chocolate, vinegar, or a candle). With your eyes closed (or blindfolded), try to guess what each smell is. Describe what each one smells like and if it is pleasant or unpleasant to you.

Activity

Scented Play Doh

Directions:

With a trusted adult, follow the directions below to make some scented Play-Doh.

1 cup flour

1 cup salt

1 cup hot water

1 tsp. Nutmeg

1 tsp. Pumpkin Pie Spice

Add all of the ingredients to a bowl. Mix it up completely until it forms a ball and is not sticky.

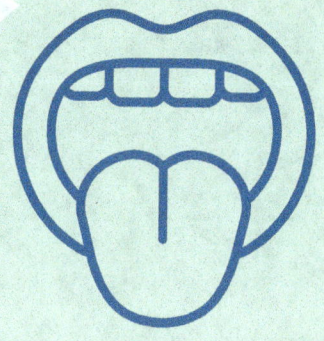

Taste

Fun Facts:

Everyone has a different number of taste buds (those tiny dots on our tongues that help us taste food).

Your sense of smell and taste work together. This is why it can be hard to taste food if your nose is stuffed up!

Foods I love to taste:

Foods I do not like to taste:

Activity
Edible Sensory Bin

Directions:
Use only edible supplies to create a sensory bin that is fun to play in and delicious! Some ideas are below:

Whipped cream
Add food coloring and practice mixing and blending with a paintbrush. Then enjoy a tasty treat!

Edible sand
Cereal and graham crackers can be crushed and blended to make sand! Add water and watch what happens.

Activity

Edible Sensory Bin

There are many different ways to make an edible sensory bin. Write your own edible sensory bin recipe down here! What did you like about it, and what didn't you like? How many different flavors did you taste?

My Edible Sensory Bin

Ingredients:

_____

_____

_____

Hearing

Fun Facts:

Your ears contain 3 of the smallest bones in your body.

The inside part of your ear helps you balance!

Earwax catches dirt and keeps it from getting into your ear, helping it stay healthy.

Noises I love to listen to:

Noises I do not like to listen to:

Activity

What's Making that Noise?

Directions:

With your eyes closed or blindfolded, have your adult use different objects around the room to make noise, and guess what it could be! Switch and have your adult guess what you are using to make noise!

Ideas:

Zipping a jacket

opening and closing a door

placing toys in baskets

Activity

Loud and Soft

Directions:

Using catalogs and magazines, cut out pictures of things that make noise. Use the pictures to make a poster with the word "loud" on one side and "soft" on the other. Which noises do you like? Which ones do you dislike?

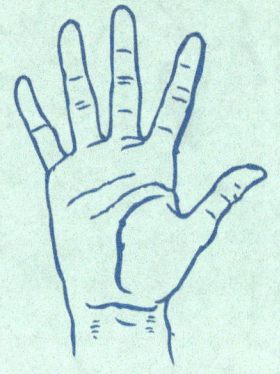

Touch

Fun Facts:

Your fingertips, lips, and toes can feel very small, gentle touches.

Touch is a way people communicate without speaking.
We hug others to show love.

Your skin is your body's largest organ.

Things I love to touch:

Things I do not like to touch:

Activity

Nature Scavenger Hunt

Directions:

Take a paper bag outside and try to fill it with as many different objects from nature as you can (leaves, flowers, branches, pinecones). Try to find things that have all different types of textures (bumpy, smooth, soft, etc.) and feel different in your hands. See if you can find everything on the list on the next page!

Activity

Nature Scavenger Hunt

☐ Soft

☐ Bumpy

☐ Smooth

☐ Hard

☐ Squishy

☐ Little

☐ Round

☐ Cold

☐ Pointy

☐ Big

Part Three

Sensory Processing

Disorder

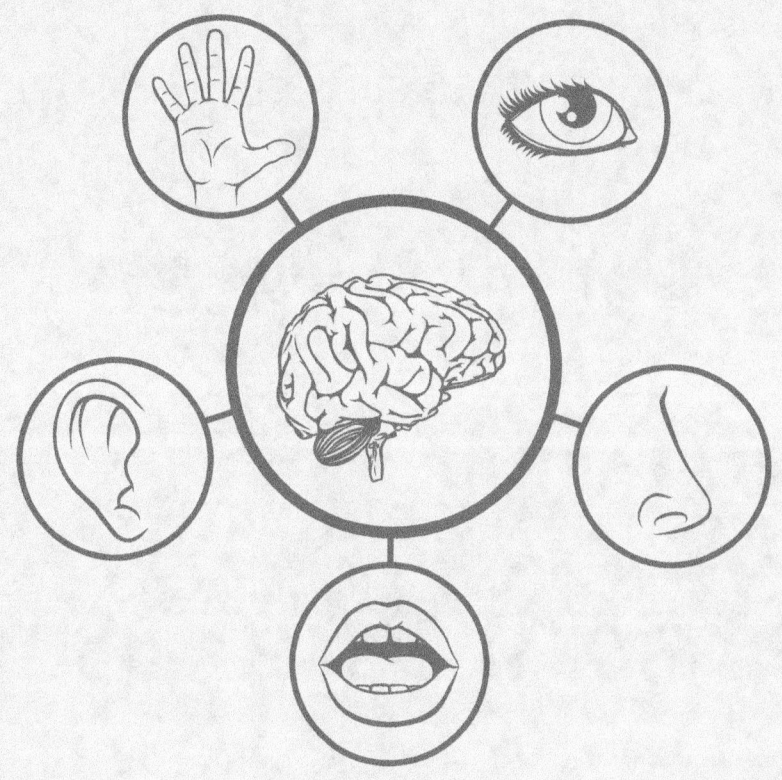

Your body sends messages to your brain about what you see, smell, taste, hear, and touch. This helps you know more about the world around you.

But sometimes, those messages can get mixed up on the way to your brain. This is called Sensory Processing Disorder, and it can be very confusing and uncomfortable for some people.

Defining Uncomfortable Sensations

When you sense (see, hear, taste, smell, touch) something you don't like, it can be very uncomfortable*. This book calls those times "having an uncomfortable sensation" but you could use other words to tell what it feels like for you.

Here are some examples:

"icky feelings"   "disgusting smells"   "terrible tastes"

*Uncomfortable is a feeling that is not very nice or pleasant. When you are uncomfortable, it is hard to relax and stay calm.

Defining Uncomfortable Sensations

What would you call your uncomfortable sensations?

_____

Whenever you see the words "having an uncomfortable sensation" in this book, you can replace them with your own words.

Below are examples of what Sensory Processing Disorder is like for some people.

"I can't stand the feeling of something sticking to me."

"I don't like to be touched or hugged."

"I am always running into or falling over things."

"I won't wear clothes that have tags."

"I have to cover my ears when I am in class. It is just too loud."

Discussion

Which senses do you think the people are talking about in the examples?

What does it feel like for you when you have an uncomfortable feeling or sensation?

Uncomfortable sensations make me feel:

(circle all that apply)

Angry	Alone
Worried	Different
Scared	Stuck
Agitated	Unique
Annoyed	Stressed
Sad	Confused
Frustrated	Hurt

This is how I feel in my body when I have uncomfortable sensations:
(circle all that apply)

Heart Pounding

Tight Muscles

Trouble Breathing

Hot and Sweaty

Jaw Clenched

_____

_____

This is how I look when I have an uncomfortable sensation

These are the thoughts in my brain when I have an uncomfortable sensation

When you have uncomfortable sensations, it can cause your brain to panic. This is called the brain's "Stress Response."
Usually, this can happen in 3 different ways: Fight, Flight, or Freeze.

Fight

anger, tantrums, yelling

Flight

panic, running away, wanting to be alone

Freeze

struggling to talk or move

Your brain goes into panic mode to help protect you. Your senses also give your brain information to protect you.

Imagine you are gathering berries. You would want your brain to let you know if the berries you smell are good, or if what you hear is an animal coming in your direction!

Sometimes, your brain might go into fight, flight, or freeze mode when it doesn't need to.

The brain's stress response happens to everyone, and everyone acts differently when their brain tells them there is danger.

When something scary or harmful happens, which way do you act?

Fight  Flight  Freeze

Can you think of a time your brain went into panic mode? Write a little bit about what happened:

_____

_____

_____

_____

_____

_____

_____

Sensory Processing Disorder can feel like a cycle

Unhelpful Thoughts
("I hate this noise!")

When I sense something uncomfortable...

Uncomfortable feelings
(mad, annnoyed)

Negative Actions
(yelling, hitting)

This is what my cycle looks like:

_____
(my unhelpful thoughts)

_____
_____
uncomfortable sensations

_____
(my uncomfortable feelings)

_____
(my negative actions)

There's nothing wrong with my body, my senses, or my brain. Everyone has sensations they like and don't like.

I'm just more sensitive.

And that's ok.

Part Four

Dealing with Unpleasant Sensations

When my brain goes into panic mode,
I can try to remember something calm

A place where
I feel relaxed

Something that
brings me peace

A list of things that make me feel calm, relaxed, and peaceful...

1.

2.

3.

4.

5.

When my senses start to send confusing messages to my brain, I can try to close my eyes and imagine these things instead.

Some other things that help me stay calm are...

Activity

5-4-3-2-1 Calming

Directions:

While taking deeps breaths, try to notice the following
things around you in as much detail as possible:

5 things you can see

4 things you can touch

3 things you can hear

2 things you can smell

1 thing you can taste

More Calming Ideas

(add your own ideas in the boxes!)

Some people might not understand why a certain sensation bothers me so much, because their senses don't work like mine.

That's ok, because I can explain it to them by telling them something simple, like...

I have super senses! I feel overwhelmed. I need a break right now.

My senses aren't the only thing about me. I am unique and special. Here are some other great things about me.

1.

2.

3.

4.

5.

My Self-Portrait

Congratulations!

You completed the workbook.

What I liked best about this book was:

_____

Part Five

Information for Parents & Caregivers

Sensory Overload

Sensory Overload can occur when one or more of your child's senses becomes overstimulated. For example, the music is too loud, the lights are too bright, or their clothes are too itchy. While most people may only be slightly agitated by these things, children who have sensory processing disorders struggle not to focus on this sensory input from their brain, making it seem amplified.

Sensory Overload

Each child is unique and has different sensory triggers. They also may respond to sensory overload in different ways.

Symptoms of sensory overload can include:

Agitation

Anxiety

Lack of Focus

Irritability

Panic Attacks

Our Brain's Biological Stress Response

When a child experiences unpleasant sensations, it can trigger the brains biological stress response called Fight, Flight, or Freeze.

Fight

anger, irritability, tantrums

Flight

panic, running away, isolating

Freeze

inability to communicate or move

Our Brain's Biological Stress Response

It is important to talk to your child about the brain's stress response system, and let them know that while what they are experiencing might be scary, confusing, or uncomfortable, it is completely normal!

Do you think your child has a tendency to react in Fight, Flight, or Freeze mode? What are some examples you have witnessed in your child's life?

Is your child Sensory Seeking or Sensory Avoidant?

Sensory Seeking Child:

Under-sensitive to sensory input.

Examples include:

Standing too close to others

Unusual Pain Tolerance

Unaware of own strength

Clumsier than other children

Can be difficult to manage behavior in a classroom setting

Hint: They may be both, depending on the situation!

Sensory Avoidant Child:

Overreacts to sensory input.

They experience sensory input more intensely than others and attempt to avoid things that are overwhelming. Examples include:

picky eating

avoiding crowds

aversion to physical touch

Helping your Sensory Seeking Child

Sensory seeking children crave more sensory input. Try incorporating activities that involve more physical activity into your daily routine like:

Yoga

Chair Resistance Bands

Fidget Toys

Helping your Sensory Avoidant Child

Sensory avoidant children are more sensitive to sensory input. Try teaching them self-soothing activities to utilize when distressed, such as:

Deep Breathing

Mindfulness or Meditation

Carrying a comfort object

Sensory Diet

If your child's sensory needs are impacting their everyday life, such as their ability to focus in school or behave at home, they may benefit from an evaluation by an occupational therapist, who can help build a "sensory diet" based on their individual needs.

A sensory diet has nothing to do with food! Rather, it is a set of prescribed strategies, tasks, and coping skills that will help your child meet their daily sensory needs. A sensory diet could include adding more sensory input, eliminating or coping with sensory overload, or a mix of both.

Check out these resources for more information on Sensory Processing Disorder:

Child Mind Institute

https://childmind.org/article/sensory-processing-issues-explained/

Sensory Processing Disorder Parent Support

https://sensoryprocessingdisorderparentsupport.com/

STAR Institute for Sensory Processing Disorder

https://sensoryhealth.org/

About the Author

Megan Menkis is a Licensed Professional Counselor and Board Certified Art Therapist. She has been practicing in PA for over 5 years and has a passion for working with children and families.

Check out her other Book:

Super Ears: My Misophonia Workbook